50 Atlantic Flavors: Canada's East Coast Recipes

By: Kelly Johnson

Table of Contents

- Lobster Rolls
- Acadian Fricot (Chicken Stew)
- Hodge Podge (Summer Vegetable Stew)
- Blueberry Grunt
- Rapée (Acadian Potato Pie)
- Jigg's Dinner (Newfoundland Boiled Dinner)
- Fish Cakes with Salt Cod
- Molasses Brown Bread
- Solomon Gundy (Pickled Herring Spread)
- Digby Scallops in Garlic Butter
- Newfoundland Toutons with Molasses
- Lunenburg Pudding
- Bakeapple (Cloudberry) Jam
- Maritime Chowder
- Bannock with Wild Berries
- Dulse Chips
- Smoked Mackerel Spread
- Flipper Pie
- Cape Breton Oatcakes
- Acadian Chicken Fricot
- Lobster Thermidor
- Scallop and Bacon Skewers
- Pea Soup with Salt Pork
- Rappie Pie
- Traditional Fish & Brewis
- Cod au Gratin
- Partridgeberry Tarts
- Mussels in White Wine Sauce
- Butter Tarts with East Coast Twist
- Fried Clams with Tartar Sauce
- Smoked Salmon on Bannock
- Rhubarb Custard Pie
- Maple Baked Beans
- Battered Haddock with Chips
- Creamed Lobster on Toast

- Cranberry Chutney
- New Brunswick Fiddlehead Salad
- Cape Breton Pork Pies
- Salt Cod Fritters
- Wild Blueberry Cobbler
- Poached Salmon with Dill Sauce
- Beothuk Bannock
- Oyster Rockefeller – East Coast Style
- Scallop Chowder
- Haskap Berry Jam
- Bar Clams in Garlic Butter
- Brown Bread with Molasses Butter
- Wild Game Meat Pie
- Maple Whiskey Glazed Salmon
- Maritime Ginger Cake

Lobster Rolls

Ingredients

- 1 lb cooked lobster meat, chopped
- 1/4 cup mayonnaise
- 1 tbsp lemon juice
- 1 tbsp chopped chives
- 1/2 tsp salt
- 1/4 tsp black pepper
- 4 New England-style split-top buns
- 2 tbsp butter, melted

Instructions

1. In a bowl, mix lobster, mayonnaise, lemon juice, chives, salt, and pepper.
2. Brush buns with butter and toast in a skillet until golden.
3. Fill buns with lobster mixture and serve.

Acadian Fricot (Chicken Stew)

Ingredients

- 1 whole chicken, cut into pieces
- 6 cups water
- 4 potatoes, diced
- 2 carrots, sliced
- 1 onion, chopped
- 1/2 tsp summer savory
- Salt and pepper to taste

Instructions

1. In a pot, bring chicken and water to a boil. Simmer for 45 minutes.
2. Remove chicken, shred meat, and return to pot.
3. Add potatoes, carrots, onion, and summer savory. Simmer until vegetables are tender.
4. Season with salt and pepper before serving.

Hodge Podge (Summer Vegetable Stew)

Ingredients

- 2 cups baby potatoes, halved
- 1 cup green beans, trimmed
- 1 cup carrots, sliced
- 1 cup yellow beans, trimmed
- 2 cups heavy cream
- 2 tbsp butter
- Salt and pepper to taste

Instructions

1. Boil potatoes until almost tender, then add beans and carrots. Cook until all vegetables are tender.
2. Drain water and add butter, cream, salt, and pepper.
3. Simmer gently for 5 minutes before serving.

Blueberry Grunt

Ingredients

- 4 cups fresh blueberries
- 1/2 cup sugar
- 1/2 cup water
- 1 tsp lemon juice
- 1 1/2 cups flour
- 2 tsp baking powder
- 1/4 tsp salt
- 3 tbsp butter
- 1/2 cup milk

Instructions

1. In a pot, simmer blueberries, sugar, water, and lemon juice for 10 minutes.
2. In a bowl, mix flour, baking powder, salt, and butter. Stir in milk.
3. Drop spoonfuls of dough into the blueberry mixture.
4. Cover and steam for 15 minutes until dumplings are cooked.

Rapée (Acadian Potato Pie)

Ingredients

- 5 large potatoes, grated
- 1/2 lb salted pork, diced
- 1/2 onion, chopped
- 1 tsp salt
- 1/4 tsp black pepper

Instructions

1. Preheat oven to 375°F (190°C).
2. Drain excess water from grated potatoes and mix with salt and pepper.
3. In a skillet, fry pork and onion until crispy.
4. Stir into potatoes and spread into a greased baking dish.
5. Bake for 2 hours until golden.

Jigg's Dinner (Newfoundland Boiled Dinner)

Ingredients

- 1 lb salt beef, soaked overnight
- 4 potatoes, peeled
- 2 carrots, peeled and sliced
- 1 turnip, diced
- 1 small cabbage, quartered
- 1/2 cup split yellow peas (optional)

Instructions

1. Boil salt beef for 2 hours, changing water once.
2. Add potatoes, carrots, turnip, and cabbage. Simmer until tender.
3. Serve with mustard pickles or gravy.

Fish Cakes with Salt Cod

Ingredients

- 1 lb salt cod, soaked overnight
- 2 cups mashed potatoes
- 1 small onion, minced
- 1 egg, beaten
- 1/2 cup flour
- 1/4 cup butter (for frying)

Instructions

1. Boil salt cod until flaky, then mix with mashed potatoes, onion, and egg.
2. Shape into patties and coat lightly with flour.
3. Fry in butter until golden on both sides.

Molasses Brown Bread

Ingredients

- 3 cups whole wheat flour
- 1 cup all-purpose flour
- 1 tbsp baking powder
- 1 tsp baking soda
- 1 tsp salt
- 1/2 cup molasses
- 1 1/2 cups buttermilk

Instructions

1. Preheat oven to 350°F (175°C) and grease a loaf pan.
2. Mix flours, baking powder, baking soda, and salt.
3. Stir in molasses and buttermilk until combined.
4. Pour into pan and bake for 50-55 minutes.

Solomon Gundy (Pickled Herring Spread)

Ingredients

- 1/2 lb pickled herring fillets
- 1 small onion, chopped
- 2 tbsp vinegar
- 1 tbsp mustard
- 1/4 tsp allspice
- 1/4 tsp black pepper

Instructions

1. Blend all ingredients until smooth.
2. Chill before serving with crackers or toast.

Digby Scallops in Garlic Butter

Ingredients

- 1 lb Digby scallops
- 2 tbsp butter
- 2 cloves garlic, minced
- 1 tbsp lemon juice
- 1 tbsp parsley, chopped
- Salt and pepper to taste

Instructions

1. Heat butter in a skillet and sauté garlic until fragrant.
2. Add scallops and cook for 2 minutes per side.
3. Drizzle with lemon juice, sprinkle with parsley, and serve.

Newfoundland Toutons with Molasses

Ingredients

- 3 cups flour
- 1 tbsp sugar
- 1 tsp salt
- 1 1/2 tsp yeast
- 1 cup warm water
- 2 tbsp butter
- Molasses for serving

Instructions

1. Dissolve yeast in warm water and let sit for 5 minutes.
2. Mix flour, sugar, and salt. Add yeast mixture and knead into dough.
3. Let rise for 1 hour, then shape into rounds.
4. Fry in butter until golden and serve with molasses.

Lunenburg Pudding

Ingredients

- 1 lb ground pork
- 1/2 cup rolled oats
- 1/2 tsp salt
- 1/2 tsp black pepper
- 1/4 tsp allspice
- 1/4 tsp cloves
- 1/4 cup onion, finely chopped
- 1/4 cup water

Instructions

1. Mix all ingredients in a bowl until well combined.
2. Shape into a loaf or stuff into a sausage casing.
3. Bake at 350°F (175°C) for 45 minutes, or steam until firm.
4. Slice and serve with mustard or molasses.

Bakeapple (Cloudberry) Jam

Ingredients

- 2 cups bakeapples (cloudberries)
- 1 cup sugar
- 1 tbsp lemon juice

Instructions

1. In a saucepan, combine all ingredients and bring to a boil.
2. Simmer for 15-20 minutes, stirring occasionally.
3. Mash slightly, then let cool before storing in jars.

Maritime Chowder

Ingredients

- 1 tbsp butter
- 1 onion, chopped
- 2 potatoes, diced
- 2 cups seafood (lobster, scallops, haddock)
- 3 cups fish stock
- 1 cup heavy cream
- 1/2 cup corn
- Salt and pepper to taste

Instructions

1. In a pot, melt butter and sauté onion until soft.
2. Add potatoes and fish stock, simmering until potatoes are tender.
3. Stir in seafood, corn, and cream, cooking until heated through.
4. Season and serve hot.

Bannock with Wild Berries

Ingredients

- 2 cups flour
- 1 tbsp baking powder
- 1/2 tsp salt
- 1/4 cup butter, melted
- 3/4 cup water
- 1/2 cup wild berries (blueberries, raspberries)

Instructions

1. Preheat oven to 375°F (190°C).
2. In a bowl, mix flour, baking powder, and salt.
3. Stir in butter and water to form a dough, then fold in berries.
4. Shape into a round loaf and bake for 25-30 minutes.

Dulse Chips

Ingredients

- 1 cup dried dulse
- 1 tbsp olive oil
- 1/4 tsp sea salt

Instructions

1. Preheat oven to 300°F (150°C).
2. Toss dulse with olive oil and spread on a baking sheet.
3. Bake for 5-7 minutes until crisp.
4. Sprinkle with salt and serve.

Smoked Mackerel Spread

Ingredients

- 1 cup smoked mackerel, flaked
- 4 oz cream cheese
- 1 tbsp lemon juice
- 1 tbsp chopped chives
- 1/2 tsp black pepper

Instructions

1. Blend all ingredients in a food processor until smooth.
2. Serve with crackers or toasted bread.

Flipper Pie

Ingredients

- 2 cups seal flipper meat, cooked and diced
- 1 onion, chopped
- 2 tbsp butter
- 1/2 cup beef broth
- 1/2 tsp thyme
- 1/2 tsp salt
- 1/4 tsp pepper
- 1 double pie crust

Instructions

1. Preheat oven to 375°F (190°C).
2. Sauté onion in butter, then add flipper meat, broth, and spices. Simmer for 10 minutes.
3. Pour into a pie crust, top with another crust, and seal edges.
4. Bake for 40-45 minutes until golden brown.

Cape Breton Oatcakes

Ingredients

- 2 cups rolled oats
- 1 cup flour
- 1/2 cup brown sugar
- 1/2 tsp salt
- 1/2 cup butter, melted
- 1/4 cup hot water

Instructions

1. Preheat oven to 350°F (175°C).
2. In a bowl, mix oats, flour, sugar, and salt.
3. Stir in butter and water until combined.
4. Roll out dough, cut into squares, and bake for 15-18 minutes.

Acadian Chicken Fricot

Ingredients

- 1 whole chicken, cut into pieces
- 6 cups water
- 4 potatoes, diced
- 2 carrots, sliced
- 1 onion, chopped
- 1/2 tsp summer savory
- Salt and pepper to taste

Instructions

1. In a pot, bring chicken and water to a boil. Simmer for 45 minutes.
2. Remove chicken, shred meat, and return to pot.
3. Add potatoes, carrots, onion, and summer savory. Simmer until vegetables are tender.
4. Season with salt and pepper before serving.

Lobster Thermidor

Ingredients

- 2 lobster tails, cooked and chopped
- 2 tbsp butter
- 1 tbsp flour
- 1/2 cup heavy cream
- 1/4 cup white wine
- 1 tsp Dijon mustard
- 1/2 cup grated cheese
- Salt and pepper to taste

Instructions

1. Preheat oven to 400°F (200°C).
2. In a saucepan, melt butter and stir in flour.
3. Add cream, wine, mustard, and cheese, stirring until smooth.
4. Fold in lobster meat, season, and spoon into lobster shells.
5. Bake for 10-12 minutes until bubbly.

Scallop and Bacon Skewers

Ingredients

- 12 large scallops
- 6 slices bacon, halved
- 1 tbsp maple syrup
- 1 tbsp olive oil
- 1/2 tsp black pepper

Instructions

1. Preheat grill to medium heat.
2. Wrap each scallop with bacon and thread onto skewers.
3. Brush with maple syrup and olive oil, then sprinkle with pepper.
4. Grill for 3-4 minutes per side until scallops are opaque.

Pea Soup with Salt Pork

Ingredients

- 2 cups dried yellow split peas
- 1/2 lb salt pork, diced
- 1 onion, chopped
- 2 carrots, diced
- 2 potatoes, diced
- 6 cups water
- 1/2 tsp thyme
- 1/2 tsp black pepper

Instructions

1. Rinse split peas and soak overnight.
2. In a pot, fry salt pork until browned. Add onion and cook until soft.
3. Pour in water and add peas, carrots, potatoes, thyme, and pepper.
4. Simmer for 1.5-2 hours, stirring occasionally.

Rappie Pie

Ingredients

- 5 lbs potatoes, grated
- 1 lb chicken, cooked and shredded
- 4 cups chicken broth
- 1 onion, chopped
- 1/2 cup butter, melted
- 1 tsp salt
- 1/2 tsp black pepper

Instructions

1. Preheat oven to 375°F (190°C).
2. Squeeze excess liquid from grated potatoes.
3. In a pot, simmer broth with onion, salt, and pepper.
4. Stir hot broth into potatoes, then layer in a greased baking dish with chicken.
5. Drizzle with butter and bake for 2 hours until golden.

Traditional Fish & Brewis

Ingredients

- 2 cups hard bread, broken into pieces
- 1 lb salt cod, soaked overnight
- 1/4 cup butter, melted
- 1 small onion, chopped
- 1/2 cup scrunchions (fried pork fat)

Instructions

1. Soak hard bread in water for 1 hour.
2. Boil salt cod until flaky, then drain.
3. In a skillet, fry scrunchions until crispy.
4. Mix fish and bread, drizzle with butter, and top with scrunchions.

Cod au Gratin

Ingredients

- 1 lb cod fillets
- 2 tbsp butter
- 2 tbsp flour
- 1 cup milk
- 1/2 cup grated cheese
- 1/2 tsp salt
- 1/4 tsp black pepper
- 1/4 cup breadcrumbs

Instructions

1. Preheat oven to 375°F (190°C).
2. In a saucepan, melt butter and stir in flour.
3. Gradually add milk, stirring until thickened.
4. Add cheese, salt, and pepper, then pour over cod in a baking dish.
5. Sprinkle breadcrumbs on top and bake for 25 minutes.

Partridgeberry Tarts

Ingredients

- 1 1/2 cups partridgeberries
- 1/2 cup sugar
- 1 tbsp cornstarch
- 1 tbsp water
- 1 tsp lemon juice
- 1 pre-made tart shell

Instructions

1. Preheat oven to 350°F (175°C).
2. In a saucepan, cook berries, sugar, and water until soft.
3. Stir in cornstarch and lemon juice to thicken.
4. Spoon into tart shells and bake for 15 minutes.

Mussels in White Wine Sauce

Ingredients

- 2 lbs mussels, cleaned
- 1 tbsp butter
- 2 cloves garlic, minced
- 1/2 cup white wine
- 1/4 cup parsley, chopped
- 1/4 tsp black pepper

Instructions

1. Melt butter in a pot and sauté garlic until fragrant.
2. Add wine and mussels, cover, and steam for 5 minutes.
3. Sprinkle with parsley and black pepper before serving.

Butter Tarts with East Coast Twist

Ingredients

- 1 cup brown sugar
- 1/2 cup maple syrup
- 1/4 cup butter, melted
- 1 egg
- 1 tsp vanilla extract
- 1/2 cup raisins or partridgeberries
- 12 pre-made tart shells

Instructions

1. Preheat oven to 375°F (190°C).
2. Whisk sugar, syrup, butter, egg, and vanilla until smooth.
3. Stir in raisins or partridgeberries and fill tart shells.
4. Bake for 15-18 minutes until golden.

Fried Clams with Tartar Sauce

Ingredients

- 1 lb clams, shucked
- 1 cup flour
- 1/2 cup cornmeal
- 1/2 tsp salt
- 1/4 tsp black pepper
- 1 egg
- 1/2 cup milk
- Oil for frying

Instructions

1. Heat oil to 350°F (175°C).
2. In one bowl, mix flour, cornmeal, salt, and pepper.
3. In another bowl, whisk egg and milk.
4. Dip clams in egg mixture, then coat with flour mixture.
5. Fry until golden and crispy.

Smoked Salmon on Bannock

Ingredients

- 2 cups flour
- 1 tbsp baking powder
- 1/2 tsp salt
- 1/4 cup butter, melted
- 3/4 cup water
- 4 oz smoked salmon
- 2 tbsp cream cheese
- 1 tbsp chopped chives

Instructions

1. Preheat oven to 375°F (190°C).
2. Mix flour, baking powder, and salt in a bowl.
3. Stir in butter and water to form a dough.
4. Shape into rounds and bake for 20 minutes.
5. Spread with cream cheese, top with smoked salmon, and garnish with chives.

Rhubarb Custard Pie

Ingredients

- 1 unbaked pie crust
- 3 cups rhubarb, chopped
- 1 cup sugar
- 2 tbsp flour
- 3 eggs
- 1/2 cup heavy cream
- 1 tsp vanilla extract

Instructions

1. Preheat oven to 375°F (190°C).
2. Spread rhubarb in the pie crust.
3. In a bowl, whisk sugar, flour, eggs, cream, and vanilla.
4. Pour over rhubarb and bake for 40-45 minutes.

Maple Baked Beans

Ingredients

- 2 cups dried navy beans
- 1/2 cup maple syrup
- 1/4 cup molasses
- 1 small onion, chopped
- 1/2 tsp salt
- 1/4 tsp black pepper
- 1/2 tsp dry mustard
- 4 cups water
- 1/2 cup salt pork or bacon, diced

Instructions

1. Soak beans overnight, then drain and rinse.
2. Preheat oven to 325°F (165°C).
3. In a pot, combine beans, maple syrup, molasses, onion, salt, pepper, mustard, and water.
4. Transfer to a baking dish, add salt pork, and bake for 4-5 hours, stirring occasionally.

Battered Haddock with Chips

Ingredients

- 4 haddock fillets
- 1 cup flour
- 1/2 cup cornstarch
- 1 tsp baking powder
- 1/2 tsp salt
- 1 cup cold soda water
- Vegetable oil for frying
- 4 large potatoes, cut into fries

Instructions

1. Heat oil to 350°F (175°C).
2. In a bowl, mix flour, cornstarch, baking powder, and salt. Whisk in soda water.
3. Dip haddock fillets into batter and fry until golden.
4. Fry potatoes until crispy.

Creamed Lobster on Toast

Ingredients

- 1 lb cooked lobster meat, chopped
- 2 tbsp butter
- 1 tbsp flour
- 1 cup heavy cream
- 1/2 tsp salt
- 1/4 tsp black pepper
- 4 slices toasted bread

Instructions

1. In a saucepan, melt butter and stir in flour.
2. Gradually add cream, stirring until thickened.
3. Stir in lobster, salt, and pepper. Simmer for 5 minutes.
4. Serve over toasted bread.

Cranberry Chutney

Ingredients

- 2 cups cranberries
- 1/2 cup sugar
- 1/2 cup apple cider vinegar
- 1/4 cup diced onion
- 1/2 tsp cinnamon
- 1/4 tsp cloves

Instructions

1. Combine all ingredients in a saucepan.
2. Simmer for 20 minutes, stirring occasionally.
3. Let cool before storing.

New Brunswick Fiddlehead Salad

Ingredients

- 2 cups fiddleheads, cleaned
- 1/2 cup cherry tomatoes, halved
- 1/4 cup red onion, sliced
- 2 tbsp olive oil
- 1 tbsp lemon juice
- 1/2 tsp salt
- 1/4 tsp black pepper

Instructions

1. Blanch fiddleheads in boiling water for 2 minutes, then rinse in cold water.
2. Toss with tomatoes, onion, olive oil, lemon juice, salt, and pepper.
3. Serve chilled.

Cape Breton Pork Pies

Ingredients

- 1 1/2 cups flour
- 1/2 cup butter, chilled and cubed
- 1/4 cup cold water
- 1/2 cup brown sugar
- 1/2 cup raisins
- 1/2 tsp cinnamon

Instructions

1. Preheat oven to 375°F (190°C).
2. Mix flour and butter until crumbly. Add cold water to form a dough.
3. Roll out dough and cut into small circles. Press into muffin tins.
4. Mix brown sugar, raisins, and cinnamon. Fill pastry cups.
5. Bake for 15-18 minutes.

Salt Cod Fritters

Ingredients

- 1 lb salt cod, soaked overnight
- 1 cup mashed potatoes
- 1/2 cup flour
- 1 egg
- 1/4 cup chopped parsley
- Oil for frying

Instructions

1. Boil salt cod until flaky, then mix with mashed potatoes, flour, egg, and parsley.
2. Shape into small fritters and fry in hot oil until golden brown.

Wild Blueberry Cobbler

Ingredients

- 4 cups wild blueberries
- 1/2 cup sugar
- 1 tbsp lemon juice
- 1 cup flour
- 1/2 cup butter, melted
- 1/2 cup milk
- 1 tsp baking powder

Instructions

1. Preheat oven to 375°F (190°C).
2. Mix blueberries, sugar, and lemon juice in a baking dish.
3. In a bowl, mix flour, baking powder, butter, and milk.
4. Drop batter over berries and bake for 35 minutes.

Poached Salmon with Dill Sauce

Ingredients

- 2 salmon fillets
- 2 cups water
- 1/2 cup white wine
- 1 tbsp lemon juice
- 1/2 tsp salt
- 1/2 cup sour cream
- 1 tbsp fresh dill, chopped

Instructions

1. Bring water, wine, lemon juice, and salt to a simmer.
2. Add salmon and poach for 10 minutes.
3. Mix sour cream and dill for sauce. Serve over salmon.

Beothuk Bannock

Ingredients

- 2 cups flour
- 1 tbsp baking powder
- 1/2 tsp salt
- 1/4 cup lard or butter
- 3/4 cup water

Instructions

1. Preheat oven to 375°F (190°C).
2. Mix flour, baking powder, and salt.
3. Cut in lard or butter, then add water to form a dough.
4. Shape into a round loaf and bake for 25-30 minutes.

Oyster Rockefeller – East Coast Style

Ingredients

- 12 fresh oysters, shucked
- 2 tbsp butter
- 2 cloves garlic, minced
- 1/4 cup shallots, finely chopped
- 1/2 cup spinach, chopped
- 1/4 cup heavy cream
- 1/4 cup breadcrumbs
- 1/4 cup grated Parmesan cheese
- 1 tbsp lemon juice
- 1/4 tsp black pepper

Instructions

1. Preheat oven to 400°F (200°C).
2. In a pan, melt butter and sauté garlic and shallots until fragrant.
3. Add spinach and cook until wilted, then stir in cream, breadcrumbs, cheese, lemon juice, and pepper.
4. Spoon mixture onto each oyster and bake for 8-10 minutes.

Scallop Chowder

Ingredients

- 1 tbsp butter
- 1 small onion, chopped
- 2 cups potatoes, diced
- 3 cups seafood stock
- 1 cup heavy cream
- 1/2 lb scallops
- 1/2 cup corn
- Salt and pepper to taste

Instructions

1. In a pot, melt butter and sauté onion until soft.
2. Add potatoes and seafood stock, simmering until potatoes are tender.
3. Stir in cream, scallops, and corn, cooking until scallops are opaque.
4. Season and serve hot.

Haskap Berry Jam

Ingredients

- 2 cups haskap berries
- 1 cup sugar
- 1 tbsp lemon juice
- 1 tsp pectin (optional)

Instructions

1. In a saucepan, mix berries, sugar, and lemon juice.
2. Simmer for 15-20 minutes, stirring frequently.
3. If using pectin, add it in the last 5 minutes.
4. Let cool before storing in jars.

Bar Clams in Garlic Butter

Ingredients

- 12 bar clams, cleaned
- 2 tbsp butter
- 2 cloves garlic, minced
- 1 tbsp lemon juice
- 1 tbsp chopped parsley
- 1/4 tsp black pepper

Instructions

1. In a skillet, melt butter and sauté garlic until fragrant.
2. Add clams and cook until they open.
3. Stir in lemon juice, parsley, and black pepper.

Brown Bread with Molasses Butter

Ingredients

- 3 cups whole wheat flour
- 1 cup all-purpose flour
- 1 tbsp baking powder
- 1/2 tsp salt
- 1/2 cup molasses
- 1 1/2 cups buttermilk

Molasses Butter

- 1/2 cup butter, softened
- 2 tbsp molasses

Instructions

1. Preheat oven to 350°F (175°C).
2. In a bowl, mix flours, baking powder, and salt.
3. Stir in molasses and buttermilk until combined.
4. Pour into a greased loaf pan and bake for 50-55 minutes.
5. Mix butter and molasses, then spread on warm bread.

Wild Game Meat Pie

Ingredients

- 1 lb ground wild game (venison, moose, or rabbit)
- 1/2 cup onion, chopped
- 1/2 cup potatoes, diced
- 1/2 cup carrots, diced
- 1/2 tsp thyme
- 1/2 tsp salt
- 1/4 tsp black pepper
- 1/2 cup beef broth
- 1 double pie crust

Instructions

1. Preheat oven to 375°F (190°C).
2. In a skillet, cook meat and onion until browned.
3. Stir in potatoes, carrots, thyme, salt, pepper, and broth. Simmer for 10 minutes.
4. Pour into a pie crust, top with the second crust, and seal edges.
5. Bake for 40-45 minutes until golden brown.

Maple Whiskey Glazed Salmon

Ingredients

- 2 salmon fillets
- 1/4 cup maple syrup
- 2 tbsp whiskey
- 1 tbsp soy sauce
- 1 clove garlic, minced
- 1/2 tsp black pepper

Instructions

1. Preheat oven to 375°F (190°C).
2. In a bowl, mix maple syrup, whiskey, soy sauce, garlic, and pepper.
3. Place salmon in a baking dish and brush with glaze.
4. Bake for 15-18 minutes, basting halfway through.

Maritime Ginger Cake

Ingredients

- 2 cups flour
- 1/2 cup brown sugar
- 1/2 cup molasses
- 1/2 cup butter, melted
- 1 tsp baking soda
- 1/2 tsp cinnamon
- 1/2 tsp nutmeg
- 1/2 tsp salt
- 1/2 cup milk
- 1 egg

Instructions

1. Preheat oven to 350°F (175°C). Grease a cake pan.
2. In a bowl, mix flour, sugar, baking soda, cinnamon, nutmeg, and salt.
3. In another bowl, whisk molasses, butter, milk, and egg. Combine with dry ingredients.
4. Pour into pan and bake for 30-35 minutes.